Become a Private Investor

By

Joseph Oppenheim

Become a Private Investor

ISBN 145281807X
EAN-13 9781452818078

Email: joeo222@aol.com

Other book by Joseph Oppenheim: Joseph's Almanac

Contents

Money

Money may not be the most important thing in life, but it is key to coping with one's life. So, not number one, but has to be remembered when making other decisions.

There is always an economic consideration to life. Even wanting to help others, money can play a part. Money plays different roles with different people. Some think of it as a form of love, either being received from others, using it as a form of self-love, or in loving others. Some think of it as a way to provide security, some to allow a degree of independence or some, as a way to help others, making the world a better place, etc. Of course, money usually serves several purposes to a person. First, you need to recognize what money means to you, then make plans on how to handle it. And, make sure you understand the priorities in which money has roles in your life.

It must be remembered that money is but a tool, a way to achieve other ends, not an end in itself. Plus, mathematics plays a part. To handle money wisely does require some basic math skills, probably not higher than an eighth grade level, but some dexterity with numbers is needed.

What is a Private Investor?

Calling oneself a private investor is when one earns one's money entirely by managing one's portfolio of investments. Also, if one could do so, but chooses to also have a vocation because of a love for doing it. So, it seems to me that even if one always intends to keep "working," by becoming a private investor, it allows the perfect environment for the person, complete independence about how to pursue the "work."

How to Become a Private Investor

There are many ways to become one, like by winning a lottery then quitting one's job then investing the money, or likewise through inheritance or another way by essentially starting with enough money. However, I'll cover the approach which is possible for basically the average person. These are steps which can work. Obviously, it could be possible to skip some of the earlier steps, depending on an individual's circumstances and how one might have altered their life's goals over the years.

One, start with a goal of wanting to be a private investor. Perhaps, like from childhood, wanting to reach an early stage in one's life where he/she no longer wants to either be an employee or be self-employed which requires running day-to-day actual operations in a business. Another way to look at it, is by owning assets where other people do the "work," per se. This is not much different from owning a business, just one step removed. In fact, Warren Buffett essentially has done that, by buying entire companies, then using the cash flow from those companies to buy other investments - like shares of stock in major companies plus holding other securities. In this case, though, I would envision a child expecting to work at a normal job, but using the cash flow to build up savings and investments in order to no longer need the job. Plus, it is an advantage to have one's job(s), and education leading up to it, serve to prepare a person, I'd say being well-versed on many things.

Two, learn that it isn't how much you earn, but how much you spend and save from what you earn, that is important. I have noticed that there basically are two kinds of people, those who never save no matter how much they earn and those who save no matter how little they earn. Sure, there may be a middle road, but rarely.

It is a mind set. Obviously, it is the latter mind set which is necessary to becoming a private investor from humble beginnings, and the sooner one can embrace that mind set the better. What goes along with that is to learn that it really is possible to enjoy life to its fullest, really very simply - public parks, home cooking, using coupons, etc, etc. In fact, it can become a pleasant challenge, in learning how to navigate such a lifestyle.

Three, start early in saving and investing, and reading about investing. Even if you have just one FDIC-insured CD and one stock, you begin to build up a knowledge of investing. Knowledge and experience are the keys. Let's say one begins as a teenager, by the time the person is in their 30's or 40's, one has maybe 20-25 years of experience and accumulated knowledge. So, targeting perhaps the mid-40's to be in a position to become a full-fledged private investor is certainly reasonable.

Four, then just follow the following chapters. It really isn't very difficult, just requires a mind set and a desire to learn.

Also, it should be remembered that if one has embraced the mind set of being able to enjoy life to its fullest while living inexpensively, one's portfolio need not be extraordinarily large.

Family

Planning one's monetary future should not be done in a vacuum, most importantly regarding one's plans for having a family. I do recommend establishing a firm financial footing before getting married and having children. I also recommend that a couple be on the same wavelength as for one or both to becoming a private investor. Financial problems have been known to be perhaps the primary cause leading to divorce, plus divorce is generally expensive itself.

Plus, women planning to become a private investor generally have the added challenge in that generally women marry younger than men so they have less single-time to establish a financial footing, also considering that women, on average, earn less at the same job as a man. A couple can actually speed the process and make it more enjoyable if they are really a team in the process. Two can live more cheaply than two single people and if they share the desire it is more fun.

General

Even if you don't follow everything in this book, I hope you take away some things to help you. Everyone is unique and life is complex with all kinds of conflicting challenges, so do remember to always think for yourself. This is a guide which can work

Investing is an Art

Even though I present an analytical look into investing, always remember it is really an art. Even with a terrific investment pick, be it stock or whatever, timing is always key and that is where contrarian thinking is helpful. It is your goal to become an expert, not to trust others no matter how popular their opinions might be. It is important to be aware of respected sources of opinions, but never to rely on them.

Therefore, I also caution an aspiring private investor to stay away from micro-managing statistics, etc associated with a particular security. For example, a company should have a strong balance sheet, the exact numbers are less important than the big picture, the totality. So, a consensus of research opinions by other experts is the important thing. This underscores my opinion that becoming a private investor isn't really difficult, stick with quality and don't worry about scouring every nook and cranny for some rare investment of which few people are aware.

Plus, my approach with this book is not to provide micro-details. Just make sure your research leads to other books, periodicals, etc to build your expertise. I'm more concerned here with developing the right mind set and general approaches. For this reason that is why this is a short book, to get you in the right mind set, not to labor you with a burdensome amount of details at this point.

The Great Recession

The recent economic turmoil, frequently called the Great Recession provides an extra incentive for a person to become a private investor. It has been said that we are in a "new normal" meaning that high unemployment may remain for many years, plus with ever-increasing global competition one must be prepared for figuring how to earn a living without depending on society providing an easy access to a job, the right job you are qualified for, etc.

Motivation

In the book, "Drive," the author Daniel Pink writes that society has evolved that to be best motivated a worker must be provided autonomy, mastery and purpose. Becoming a private investor achieves those goals. Autonomy is achieved because one is completely without a boss. Even if one owns their own business there are still customers to please, so customers effectively become a business owner's boss. As for mastery, a private investor is always in the process of perfecting the craft. And, for purpose, besides the main purpose of providing one's living, a private investor is free to choose whatever larger purpose his/her efforts have, perhaps selecting the most moral and ethical of investments, leaving assets to a charity, etc. So, now on with things.

Optimism

Be optimistic. One might think a pessimistic attitude is better suited to prepare a person to wisely plan for the future, but I disagree. To be successful is multi-dimensional and involves many things, not just having enough money, as I mentioned at the beginning of this chapter. Being cautious, I think, goes along with being optimistic. It is like wearing a seatbelt when driving a car. You can still drive a car looking ahead for good things to happen, but you just reduce the odds against something bad happening. As I mentioned, math is part of the approach in being successful with money, and here again it really is pretty simple, but numbers do count. Plus, anecdotally, whenever I see someone who has lived a long life, they usually are cheerful people.

Mistakes

It is OK to make mistakes. The key is to learn from them and reduce the chances of making the same ones again and making others. Think of it as being an educational experience. Part of being successful involves taking risks and risk does involve chances for errors. So, it is all about balance, taking reasonable risks but also using experience from previous errors to improve chances for success.

Savings

To me, the greatest economist was Benjamin Franklin, with his "a penny saved is a penny earned." If there is one thought more important than any in this book it is to save.

Beware of any person who promises some short cut to becoming financially well-off. It really is all about saving. The risk aspect involved with investing should be only for reasonable returns, maybe by beating inflation by a few percentage points. The real way to achieve terrific returns is by getting reasonable returns while constantly adding savings to the mix. Also, beware of anyone touting some latest, new way of thinking. Stick to the basics.

Further, keep in mind when spending money, if you budget $20 to buy something and what you buy is listed at $40 with a sales price of $20 advertised as "save 50% or save $20," if you buy it you haven't saved anything. You have spent the full amount you budgeted. Saving would be if the product was listed for $20 and discounted to $10, and you bought that and put the other $10 of your budgeted amount into your savings account for eventual investment.

A Kicker

For everything in life, including investing, I always look for what I call a "kicker," something extra which increases the chances for success and/or reduces the chances for failure, or just adds something beyond the main goal(s). Let's say you are looking for a job. Maybe one job pays a little less but is located in a place which is also a place where people come to vacation - with many fun things to do and great weather - I would say it has a kicker. Same with investing. Some investments protect against inflation, some against deflation, but there are also some which protect against both even if they don't offer bigger rewards. This "kicker" is really a built-in hedge or diversification. I like the word, kicker.

It is also good to get in the habit of recording every purchase you make. Ideally, carrying along a notepad with you or some kind of mobile computing device, smart phone, etc. At least at the end of every day, record somewhere what purchases you made. If you want to exclude extremely small outlays, that is OK, but having such a habit does at least exert some control over your spending, since you know there is some extra step involved so you might think twice about making such a purchase.

Panic and Greed

Always be on guard for getting greedy or panicking. Financial markets reflect human emotions, mainly panic or greed. The best decisions usually come when the masses are either panicking or getting greedy. One of my mottos is you never lose money by taking a profit. Never be afraid of missing a top or bottom exactly. I also call it being flexible. Never get caught up with emotions. Be ready to react when opportunity presents itself.

Quality

I always recommend sticking with quality, with everything, especially with investments. There is a reason I mention this in the chapter, "Mind Set." That way, you will never be caught with garbage, so to speak. Let's say you dabble in risky, more speculative things, and something drastic happens - maybe you get injured or sick and someone else has to take over your finances or a natural disaster happens - you simply don't want to be in a situation where at a critical time you are at a severe disadvantage.

Plus, this also fits in with not being greedy, plus it has the extra "kicker," quality is always in demand. If you are forced to sell something there is always some premium for quality.

Be Flexible

Always be alert to take advantage of an opportunity which presents itself, even if it diverges from your plan, as long as you still are following the main purpose of the plan. For example, if there is a bargain for some food item which you don't currently need and isn't perishable, go ahead and take advantage of the bargain and stock up on the item. You should always have a reserve account, savings, etc which permits you to take advantage of such situations. Same with investments, a stock market collapse, etc might present opportunities to use such reserves. Same in the reverse, if prices seem high for something, be prepared to skip such a purchase and either substitute something else or pass on it and wait for a better deal.

Negotiation

Just about everything is negotiable. Approach everything that way, whether it be a consumer item or investment. Think of it as a win-win situation for both you and the other party. The other party wants your business, even with a discount there is still room for them to profit and they want you to be satisfied, either because you might be a repeat customer or spread a good word about them to others. Plus, if you are clever you can even make a greater profit for them, like offering to buy a larger amount, maybe two instead of one, with each one costing less but the seller earning more on the total sale. Always just ask. Asking can be as simple as "is there a way for me to save on the product?"

Double-check Everything Financial

I cannot over-emphasize this. Whenever money is involved, always double-check whatever you do or whatever someone else does for you. Don't forget, most financial workers you interface with are low-wage employees, however this applies to anyone on the other end of a financial deal. Your goal is to know a whole lot about what you do, so as not to be overmatched in financial dealings. Your goal is to be a private investor, an expert at what you do. Whenever you give instructions, always repeat them before exiting the transaction, to make absolutely sure they were understood correctly. Plus, it even refreshes in your own mind that the instructions were correct. Never be afraid of coming across as being annoying or naive, double-checking is always wise where money is involved.

Debt

Simply said, stay away from debt. Debt is dangerous. Banks make money from it, so you might as well act as your own bank. Remember when banks, or other businesses, do fail it is almost always related to having too much debt and not enough capital. Your goal should always to be well-capitalized, having enough liquid cash to avoid going into debt. Sure, there are certain situations where some debt is OK, but only for a home, emergency health care and education, in my opinion. I only recommend credit cards if you pay the bills when due to avoid any finance charges. They do offer convenience and those which have cash rewards are great, often essentially getting a 1% or so discount for every purchase. However, if a credit card makes you spend more, forget it, except maybe for an emergency backup. I repeat, debt is dangerous.

Trust Yourself

No one cares more about your money than you. Only save or invest in what you understand. If all you understand is a government-insured savings account, that is fine. Look to build your knowledge of other investment vehicles by learning for yourself. Just take small steps to build up a knowledge. NEVER trust anyone else for investment advice. Not even me. It is all about learning for yourself. If I am able to give you ideas for further thought and research by you, great. If there if one lesson to learn from the Bernie Madoff fraud, is never trust anyone else for investment advice, no matter what others say. Think for yourself.

General Approach to Becoming a Private Investor

I have covered the initial steps in becoming a private investor in the Introduction. Here, I will go into my general approach to investing. These are the classes of assets which I suggest can make up private investor's portfolio. This portfolio will be built over time, beginning simply then expanding it as one develops experience and knowledge.

1. Stocks - individual US stocks, preferably on the NY stock exchange.

2. Bonds - US Treasury bills, notes and bonds, GNMA collateralized debt obligations, and US savings bonds.

3. CDs - FDIC (Banks) or NCUA (Credit Unions) insured certificates of deposits.

4. Precious metals - Gold - preferably coins. Silver - preferably pre-1965 90% silver coins, US Eagles and bullion.

5. Real Estate - Home(s).

Although there are many other forms of investment products, I do believe it is best to keep a simple approach like this because there really isn't a need to have anything more complex. As I say, stick with what you know best and become an expert on that, sticking always with quality.

Investments as a Business

Look at all investments, not just stocks, as if owning a business or businesses. They should return regular streams of income while also offering some moderate potential for growth and capital appreciation, except for CDs.

Avoid Middlemen

Certainly some middlemen, intermediaries, are needed, like a broker to buy, sell and hold securities, a bank for CDs, etc, however the less you use them the better. If you want stocks, buy individual ones. Don't use mutual funds, exchange traded funds (ETFs), options, or other forms of derivatives. They all involve extra costs, plus one or more steps removed from understanding what is being done. As for using them as hedges, only use diversification of the basic assets. In any financial transaction it is always wise to either know more than the other side of the deal, or at least be as close to understanding the deal as the other side as possible.

Mutual funds, on average, deliver worse returns than individual stocks. It is hard enough to navigate the world of stocks, without adding navigation of the thousands of mutual funds to the complexity which also adds to the risk of encountering crooks. Investing is an art. Stick with what you know or with minimal risks in order to build up knowledge.

Also, stay away from new products, because they always involve some extra middleman. Plus, too many times the reason for new products is to avoid existing regulations, favor older, more tested products. For example, though I don't recommend mutual funds, ETFs may seem like a better choice because of reduced commissions, however mutual funds are better regulated than ETFs. The same with hedge funds, etc, basically unregulated vehicles. With investing, experience is your friend.

Insured Investments

Don't underestimate the value of US government insurance for investing products, including savings, checking and money market accounts. And, always stay within the limits of the insurance, even if that means having separate accounts at different institutions. Being a private investor involves devoting time. Convenience is nice, but never secondary to protecting your money. For security brokerage accounts stay within the SIPC (Securities and Investor Protection Corporation) limits, even if that means opening accounts with more than one brokerage. I'll cover it later, but that is one reason I only recommend US government backed fixed income securities. Use government insurance when it is available.

Diversification

A private investor should build in diversification into one's assets. Important is to protect against both deflation and inflation. Also key is to protect against catastrophic events, usually with an adequate savings reserve along with the proper insurance which concentrates on protection against catastrophic events.

Preservation of Capital

Preservation of capital should be the most important goal of a private investor. Risk is fine, but only when it is measured and reasonable with as many protections against net worth wipe-out, like those mentioned above. Avoid what I call the "machismo" approach to investing - willing to take extreme risks in the hope of big returns. Think more along the tortoise rather than the hare approach.

Remember Bernie Madoff

The most important lesson from the Bernie Madoff Ponzi scheme, the largest financial fraud in history, is not to trust others without doing due diligence and building in enough diversification into one's assets. He was known as "Uncle Bernie" and both promised and delivered consistently high returns even during bad economic times. Plus, he rewarded everyone connected with him, including making his customers his best sales people because he would frequently reward referrals with commissions, a kind of shared greed where everyone was happy so even if there were suspicions no one was motivated to either dig deeper or bring in authorities.

Retirement Assets

Retirement assets like IRAs, 401Ks, company pension plans, Social Security, etc should be used to their maximum during one's wealth-building years. Social Security is important, particularly because it has the kicker where benefits are annually adjusted for inflation, so when one does have a job it is best to be aware of how well you are building your Social Security account. Learn as much as you can about how Social Security works

Savings

It is important to have liquid savings for emergency purposes, frequently six month's of income is recommended. I would advise being on the high side, even more than six months. Plus, since you are on the path to becoming a private investor, you do want to have cash reserves ready to take advantage of a timely investment situation which may present itself unexpectedly.

Checking, savings, and money market accounts qualify, US government-insured ones. The only exception is if using a securities brokerage account money market account, only use one which contains US Treasury short-term vehicles like Treasury bills or sometimes they offer FDIC- insured bank savings vehicles. Plus, as with anything, look for a "kicker," something extra which adds value, maybe a free safe deposit box, higher interest rate, etc. Also, by laddering CDs - having multiple long term CDs with staggered maturity dates, where one is always coming due within a year or so, plus each having reasonable or low early withdrawal penalties, this is a good way to have a savings alternative which allows one to have less money in low interest checking accounts, etc.

Certificates of Deposit

I regard US government-insured certificates of deposits (CDs) as the foundation for all prudent private investors. Many wrongly assume them to not be investments, but they are since they have a long-term aspect to them. I only recommend such CDs from banks or credit unions. Plus, I prefer ones with fixed rates attached to them. You know what you will get, plus variable rates add a degree of speculation and I don't think wise with CDs. Plus, they are available without paying a commission, an extra "kicker" I always like. Security brokerages sometimes offer CDs, but I advise staying away from them. They are brokered-CDs and violate one of my maxims, to stay away from middlemen as much as possible.

Early Withdrawal Penalties

I only recommend CDs with low or reasonable early withdrawal penalties associated with them. I won't give specific limits on what they should be because they would depend on what are the interest rates of the CDs since the penalties are based on them. Low early withdrawal penalties give CDs the added "kicker" of besides protecting against deflation which all CDs do, the low or reasonable penalty also gives them some protection against inflation since you could easily exit a CD to get a higher-paying one when inflation spikes.

Laddering

Laddering CD's involves having several CD's with maturation dates varying so one comes due every year or so, for example. That way, you are additionally protected from changing interest rates or other changing financial situations. My advice is usually to go for the highest rate, even if it means a longer term, as long as the early withdrawal penalty isn't unreasonable. Then, do they same thing the next time, meanwhile other CD's are closer to their maturities, thereby you are building in a laddering over time, but still having higher rates with all your CD's. Well-structured laddering also reduces the need for the amount you need in lower-interest rate savings vehicles, if a CD is coming due soon.

Shop Around

Since I only advise US government insured CD's, I also advise shopping around for the best rates wherever they are. Look for ads, specials, web sites like bankrate.com, magazines, etc. Don't be afraid to call different institutions from a list you keep, of potential institutions for favorable rates. And, always negotiate. Sometimes rates are negotiable or there are special deals like a higher rate if you have another account with them, etc. As I have said, negotiating is always a good habit, so that it becomes an automatic step with every financial deal.

Stocks

There are several reasons to own stocks. We are a capitalistic nation, so the government will always structure laws to help stocks, particularly favorable tax policies like for capital gains and sometimes even with dividends.

With all investments, but particularly with stocks, as I've mentioned before, think of yourself as a businessperson, that is only own stocks of companies which you would like to own completely if you could. As such, I would want to own a business which offers products or services which will always be in demand in good times or bad. Plus, the products or services are top quality ones and the company is recognized as a great one in its industry. Plus, the company must have a sterling balance sheet, preferably with little or no debt. And, like any business I might own, it must regularly return a good income to me by way of a good dividend which ideally the company regularly raises annually. Hence, one is protected, to a degree, against both deflation and inflation. Obviously, the stock would also offer a reasonable chance of capital appreciation, by way of having a business which offers reasonable growth prospects.

Also, key to stock holdings, are that they must be managed, often adding or subtracting to/from positions as situations merit. Plus, although the goal is to hold a stock forever, as one would a business, a serious adverse situation which faces a company could warrant closing out the position in the stock.

As for speculation, the only way I think it is OK is to buy more of a stock I already own or want to own long-term, thinking it might move up for a short term gain, however since it is a stock I already want to own, worst case is that if it doesn't go up right away, I just have added to my position at what I think is a cheap price. So, essentially it is a win-win kind of bet, especially as I always recommend keeping some cash in reserve - never being in a situation where I am overloaded with stocks. It should always be remembered that deep and prolonged bear markets are always possible, so stocks by their nature do carry risk. However, one other benefit of considering such trades, is that it keeps the investor more current on stock and market situations, thereby keeping one more informed. Staying informed is key. Plus, since stocks do carry risk I recommend only keeping at most about 15% of one's net worth in stocks. Many so-called experts advise greater percentages, however I put a heavier value on capital preservation than most. 15% is a guideline. My major point here is to think on the low side, rather than over-investing in stocks.

Plus, I only want to own companies which I think are in moral businesses. Not tobacco, etc. By doing so, I get some additional feelings of satisfaction. Since there are thousands of stocks from which to pick, I don't see that as a disadvantage. How you approach this is up to you.

Watch List

Always keep a list of stocks you don't own but you like. Then monitor these stocks for potential purchase.

Only US Stocks

I recommend only US stocks. The reason for this is because I think it is best to stick with what you know best. Assuming you are an American, you know American laws better, same with politics and just about everything else. Sure, you want to educate yourself beyond our borders, but with money on the line I say stick with what you know best especially when there are two sides to every trade so it just doesn't make any sense to me to increase your chances of being out-matched on the other end of a trade.

Stock-picking is an Art

It is very important to understand that picking stocks and deciding when to add or subtract from positions in them is an art. For example, one strategy is the contrarian approach, where frequently there is a tendency for a stock to either be popular or unpopular at precisely the wrong time. So, it takes a certain ability to think for yourself. The best way to evaluate your ability with stocks is to start modestly and see how you do. If you consistently don't do well, it is best to stay away from stocks altogether. They simply are not necessary.

Sample Portfolio

This is my portfolio as of publication. I only list this as a guide to the way I think. Remember, everyone is different and this should only be a guide.

KMB (Kimberly Clark)
PEP (Pepsi)
MMM (3M Corp)
PG (Procter & Gamble)
SYY (Sysco)
ADP (Automatic Data Processing)
KFT (Kraft)
BMY (Bristol Myers Squibb)

KO (Coca Cola)
T (AT&T)
GPC (Genuine Parts Company)

Bonds

I only advise US Treasury bills, notes and bonds and US government fixed income products like Government National Mortgage Association (GNMA) collateralized home loans, also known as Ginnie Maes, which are backed by the full faith and credit of the US government, and also US savings bonds. I'm not big on municipal bonds, even with their tax advantages. They simply are a too-complicated field to navigate. Plus, interest on US Treasury bonds, bills and notes aren't taxable by states and localities, so they do have some built-in tax advantages. A special mention of US Treasury Inflation Protected Securities (TIPS) is important. They are Treasury notes and bonds which offer both protection against deflation and moderate protection against inflation.

I also advise to stick with middle term or shorter bonds. My rule of thumb would be to stick with a maximum of five years until maturity. But, beware because CDs with low or reasonable early withdrawal penalties offer better protection if interest rates rise. For TIPS, though, going long term is no problem since you are protected on both the down and up side for inflation as interest rates usually follow inflation. I also recommend buying bonds which are selling below their face/maturity price. This means you can never lose anything if you hold to maturity, plus if it reaches the maturity price before maturity, it usually is a time to consider selling to generate a capital gain.

US Savings Bonds

Savings bonds also deserve a mention. The negative is that there are usually limits into how much you can buy each year. So, for moderate amounts of money they work fine, in fact better for some purposes. For one, you don't have to pay any taxes until the bonds are cashed in. Second, I think they are good instead of 529 plans which are used for funding a youth's future college expenses. You can choose regular savings bonds or inflation-protected ones.

A Home

Owning a home is fine, but not necessary. Look at it first as a consumer item, second as partially an investment. See it also as a long term commitment since if you think there is a risk you might have to move in the short term, you might be stuck when trying to sell when market conditions are poor, plus short term costs like commissions, mortgage fees, etc might not have had a long enough time to be outweighed by the capital appreciation or other anticipated benefits of the home. One should also be aware of the price of homes in an area relative to rental costs. Generally, it is just a better financial situation to rent if the average homes in an area are more than ten times the annual cost of rents for a similar home. On the other hand, sometimes buying is better from a financial standpoint. Further, the most important factor in determining whether to buy a specific home, is "location, location, location." Never sacrifice for a good location, even if that means having to buy a smaller home than one would like. Never be forced to buy. Renting is just fine. The most important investment aspect to owning is that it offers some protection from inflation. So, if you do rent, make sure you have enough inflation protection built into your other assets. Second homes are to be avoided, except as a pure consumer item. I recommend living in a place where others want to vacation. Call this a "kicker" which reduces a desire to have a vacation home. This gets back to having the right mind set of a private investor. If you do reach a wealth level where such a purchase is easily handled, fine, but not during the wealth-building years.

Rental Property

The only real estate investments I recommend are rental properties. This fits with my investing approach to treat investments as a business which always return a constant stream of income. But, remember, unlike stocks, bonds, CDs, etc, rental homes require much time to manage. Using a property manager might work, but that involves extra costs, plus worries about how effective the property manager is, therefore much oversight is still needed even if using a property manager. And, remember the ten times the annual rents rule I just mentioned. It is valuable when assessing whether a potential rental property is at a good price for investment purposes.

Precious Metals

I only recommend gold and/or silver, not other commodities or jewelry, diamonds, etc. The main reason is for portability and easy liquid conversion. Diamonds have a special purpose, in countries where insurrection is a risk, because of easy portability, but not generally for one's asset portfolio because they are hard to value, which complicates purchasing and selling. The main reason for precious metals is for an insurance policy against the currency, plus a protection from inflation. Since they aren't real investments because they don't return a stream of income, I only recommend that they constitute a small part of one's portfolio, maybe 5% maximum.

Gold

Here, US gold Eagle coins or other standard gold coins like South African Krugerrands are best. They have easy liquidity.

Silver

I see the best as pre-1965 US 90% silver coins, with silver bullion a second choice, the best being 100 ounce bars. The coins have the added "kicker" that they have a face value, so they can never go to zero in value as long as the currency still exists, plus can be used for directly buying things.

Track Expenses

If nothing else, use a journal to list all spending. Best is to use a computer program like Quicken. The free web site, Mint.com can also work They also offer many helpful features including keeping track of all your investments and monetary accounts like credit cards, etc, plus a snapshot of your total net worth at any time. Net worth is arguably the most important number of all and therefore keeping track of it paramount.

Taxes

Computer programs like H&R Block or TurboTax are excellent. Plus, stay on top of current tax laws/changes and your own tax situation. Such programs are good at that. Even if you have your tax preparation done professionally, don't take so many shortcuts that you don't keep up with things for you situation. Strive to becoming an expert at your own taxes. As for keeping track of security sales for tax purposes, there are some tools like Gainskeeper which may be helpful for you, however I do recommend keeping the amount of trades down to a manageable level, so I think if you feel you need such a tool, it is probably a warning to your investing approach. However, if you are computer savvy and you portfolio grows large, such a tool can be helpful.

File Cabinet

Key here, is too stay organized with your financial records.

Safe Deposit Box

This is important for keeping important papers, plus as for investments, precious metals, be they coins or bullion pieces.

Estate-Planning Lawyer

This is important for drawing up wills, trust documents, powers of attorney documents, etc. It is important to stay aware of the subjects via books, etc and also computer programs are helpful, but you should also have such a lawyer.

Securities Broker

For stocks and bonds, having a securities broker is a must. I recommend an on-line discount broker. One of my most important part of becoming a private investor, is to keep transaction costs low. Even if not computer savvy, there are discount brokers which are also cheap. But, remember, you should be making all the investment decisions. Stay away from relying on brokers for advice, other than to explain some technical things relating to the basics of what you need to do.

Advice

Books, magazines, and TV channels like CNBC are important to keep you alert to what is happening. Plus, I also recommend Yahoo Finance as an inexpensive way to research companies for potential investment and management. Some on-line brokers are better than others for the research features they provide. Some are excellent, yet also inexpensive. But, here again, you are to become your own expert. Stick only to what you understand, eventually building up a knowledge of various investments.

Rule of 72

This is a simple but very important tool. Take 72 and divide it by the interest rate of a financial product and the result is the approximate length of years it will take for the investment to double in value. This is so important with which to quickly understand an investment's potential, plus to see how your net worth is likely to grow.

Track Performance

Do have an organized approach to tracking how your investment portfolio is doing. I recommend a system where you know at all times your current net worth. Quicken or Mint.com work well for that since they involve setting up accounts for each asset, credit card, etc.

Debt is Dangerous

As I have mentioned, stay away from debt. Some is OK for a home, for medical emergencies, possibly education, and it is convenient with regard to a credit card as long as it is paid off each month. However, the most important goal for a private investor is preservation of capital, to not lose what you have worked so hard to accumulate. Using debt for investments is really speculation, basically guessing on the future value of an asset. The only speculation I think is OK is with managing a stock portfolio, making short term bets on stocks you already plan to hold long term. If you like to speculate, do it this way and never with debt. Plus, since banks are profitable, best to be your own bank, so to speak. Always keep enough in reserves to finance opportunities which may come up.

Self-Insured

My recommendation is to always approach insurance from the perspective of wanting to be self-insured. Like with banks, the insurance industry is profitable, so best to be your own insurance company as much as reasonable. Sure, car, home, medical, etc insurance are necessary because of potential catastrophic risks. So, my approach is to just protect against catastrophic events with high deductibles, while also keeping good cash reserves. Plus, having long term assets like stocks, bonds and CDs with modest early withdrawal penalties should keep you liquid enough to meet most modest unanticipated disruptions.

Liability Umbrella

I really recommend having a Liability Umbrella insurance policy. Our society is very litigious so best to be prepared for some unexpected expensive lawsuit against you.

Life and Disability Insurance

Obviously they are important especially when your net worth hasn't yet reached a significant amount. Here again, best to look to eventually be self-insured, so only go for the least expensive, most directed forms of such insurance. Stay away from such which also have so-called investment aspects to them. Plus, if you currently work for a major company or government agency, there are usually free or inexpensive policies provided, so do take advantage of them.

Annuities

I say stay away from them. Best to be self-insured as much as possible. Plus, annuities are complicated. Insurance companies hire actuaries to devise the mathematical algorithms behind them with the goal of making the insurance companies profits. That is another rule I have, to stay as simple as possible and stay away from middlemen as much as possible.

Spending

Just as important as investing and saving is to have a disciplined approach to spending. Remember that if one is budgeting ten dollars to spend on something and buys something normally selling at twenty dollars for ten, one has not saved anything, as I have explained in a previous chapter, "Mind Set."

Sales, Coupons, etc

Always key to savings is to spend wisely using sales, coupons, etc and always look to negotiate.

Taxes

Understand taxes, but stay away from tax schemes. Look at taxes as a "kicker," something which makes an investment or purchase a better deal, but do not use taxes as a primary motivation. It has always perplexed me why people fall for the concept of charitable remainder trusts which allow a person to give away assets in return for a tax deduction and receiving income from the assets during the rest of one's life. The way I see them is a scheme to give away your assets, all under the guise of avoiding taxes.

Charity

There have been studies showing that the amount of money people give to charity is based more on guilt than concerns for others. I don't say this to demean the concept of charity, but to see it from the right perspective. Plus, since this is a book about becoming a private investor, that is the main focus here. So, the way I think it can be handled best is to offer your time and labor as the recommended way. That's the "kicker" here. Plus, unused items like old clothes, etc make for good donations with the added benefit being the tax deductibility aspect to them. That is another reason I advocate taking a moral approach to investment choices. Since tobacco kills many thousands each year in the US, avoid such investments.

It is wise to keep stocks out of tax-deferred accounts like IRA's, 401K's, etc. That is because stocks inherently have their own tax advantages like favorable treatment for long-term capital gains, tax write-offs for capital losses and sometimes favorable tax treatment for dividends. So, such accounts are best for CD's and similar income vehicles. But, also not for bonds, since there is also favorable tax treatment for capital gains or losses with bonds. Plus, since I recommend US Treasuries for one's bond portfolio, they are already exempt from state and local taxes.

Although it is important to weigh tax consequences in timing investment buying and selling decisions, they should be secondary to whether such a decision is fundamentally sound or not.

Now Get Started

It's never too soon. As I have said, it is a mind set. If you just begin by controlling spending better and saving more for emergencies, you are on your way. Then, just take a step at a time with what you understand the best, building up your portfolio of assets and learning more all along the way. Do stay with quality and be organized, keeping track of everything and have some sort of plan. Plus, have fun and if anyone questions you about your new direction, just say you are becoming a private investor.

Notes

Feel free to use the next blank pages to write in your personal notes which you take away from this book or this book might have triggered in your thinking as you begin your journey.

Conclusion

Conclusion

Conclusion